IGUANA

The Ultimate Guide To Iguana Care, Feeding, Housing, Training (Complete Iguana Information)

Amani Barton

Table of Contents

CHAPTER ONE

Iguana

What exactly is an iguana?

Iguanas verdes are huge lizards with stunning appearances that may be found throughout the Americas. In spite of their common moniker, green iguanas may really be found in a variety of hues and subspecies. Their hue may vary from green to lavender, crimson, orange, black, and even a blackish tone with a reddish brown tint. They may also have a bluish hue and have prominent blue patterns on their bodies. Iguanas verdes have a row of spines down their backs and along the length of their tails, which serves to defend them from being eaten by other animals. Iguanas, like many other species of lizards, have the ability to break off their tails if they are being held by the tail in order to free themselves and subsequently grow a new one. Their tails have a whip-like appearance and may be used to administer terrible blows. Iguanas, like other reptiles, have a well-developed dewlap, which allows them to maintain a consistent body temperature. Courtship rituals and territorial displays both include the usage of this dewlap.

Green iguanas may sometimes have a bluish hue, and youngsters may have brown markings that are banded or blotchy in appearance. Adults usually have a single, consistent hue, and as they age, they get deeper, nearly brown in appearance. A person's skin tone might shift depending on their mood, the climate, their overall health, or even their social standing. Males endure greater color changes than females. Their spiky crest, which begins at the base of their neck and extends all the way down to the tip of their tail, is another distinguishing characteristic of this species. They also have huge cheek scales behind their ear membranes and a loose flap of skin on their neck called a dewlap that helps them regulate their body temperature. Last but not least, in the centre of the top of their skull is a parietal eye, which is the third eye that they have. This does not serve the purpose of vision; rather, it is employed for the sensing of light above them and the control of hormones.

The natural habitat of green iguanas includes the Caribbean islands of Grenada, Aruba, Curacao, Trinidad and

Tobago, St. Lucia, and St. Vincent, as well as central Brazil, the Dominican Republic, Paraguay, and Bolivia. Their native range begins in southern Mexico and extends to the center of Brazil, the Dominican Republic, Paraguay, and Bolivia. They are now native to Grand Cayman, Puerto Rico, the state of Texas, the state of Florida, the state of Hawaii, and the United States Virgin Islands. These lizards are native to tropical rain forests and may often be found in close proximity to bodies of water. They are also known to inhabit different ecosystems, such as gallery forests, dry forests, and mangrove swamps, among others. Iguanas that live on land have a broad, rounded skull and pleurodont teeth (Having the teeth attached by their sides to the inner side of the jaw, as in some lizards). Its trunk is much less in length compared to its tail. In point of fact, these innocuous lizards are still around today, although they are in risk of extinction in their original habitat.

Both the 'Conolophus subcristatus' and the 'Conolophus pallidus' species of Land Iguana may be found in the Galapagos Islands; however, the 'Conolophus pallidus' is endemic to just the island of Santa Fe. Both species of Land Iguana can be found on Santa Fe. They are more colorful than its relatives, the Marine Iguana, due to the yellowish-orange coloration of their bellies and the brownish-red coloration of their backs. They are longer than one meter (three feet) and the males of the species weigh 13 kilos each.

Land Iguanas call the drier parts of the islands their home, and in the mornings you may see them lazing about under the scorching tropical sun. On the other hand, in order to obtain some relief from the heat of the noon sun, they look for the shade provided by cacti, boulders, trees, or other types of flora.

They sleep in burrows that they have excavated in the dirt throughout the night in order to keep their body heat contained. A remarkable relationship is seen between Darwin's Finches and Land Iguanas, in which the iguanas raise themselves off the ground and enable the finches to pick off any ticks that they find.

Land iguanas get the majority of their nutrition from low-growing plants and shrubs, including the cactus, as well as fruit that has fallen to the ground and cactus pads, which may include the plant's spines. During the extended periods of drought, the nutrients and moisture that they need may be obtained from these succulent plants.

Iguanas that live on land may attain sexual maturity anywhere between 8 and 15 years of age. Males have a strong sense of territory, which drives them to actively defend certain regions, which often include more than one female. During territorial displays, animals will rapidly nod their heads and, on occasion, engage in bouts that entail biting and tail-thrashing.

Following the time of mating, the female iguanas will relocate to regions that are appropriate for nesting, and once there, they will deposit anywhere from two to twenty-five eggs in a burrow that has been excavated in the sandy soil. The female will stand guard over the burrow for a brief period of time in order to deter any other females from laying their eggs there.

After three to four months, the baby iguanas begin to hatch, but it takes them approximately a week to burrow their way out of the nest. Land iguanas have the potential to live for more than 50 years, but only if they make it through the first few challenging years of their lives, when food is often sparse and there is a threat from predators.

Saving energy by moving more slowly is an essential component of the adjustment necessary for living in a drier climate. Because of this, the animals come out as being either unintelligent or lazy. Iguanas on land create underground tunnels by burrowing into the earth. These tunnels provide the iguanas a location to breed, as well as shade during the day and safety at night.

When Charles Darwin went to the Galapagos Islands in 1835, he wrote on how numerous the land iguanas were there. However, whalers and settlers began traveling to the Galapagos Islands in the early 1800s, and they brought a variety of domestic animals with them. These included goats, pigs, dogs, cats, and other creatures. These creatures eventually ran away or were abandoned, which had devastating consequences over time. Iguana kits are preyed upon by cats, while adults are taken out by dogs. Iguanas are dependent on certain patches of plants for their sustenance, but goats clear out such areas completely. Darwin wrote about the many iguanas that lived on Santiago Island, but such iguanas no longer exist today. They have almost completely disappeared from several of the other islands.

CHAPTER TWO

Detailed explanation of the body

Iguana hatchlings may weigh as little as 12 grams, but by the time they are adults, they can weigh one kilogram (de Vosjoli, 1992). The length of a green iguana during hatching may vary anywhere from 17 to 25 centimeters. The majority of adult iguanas weigh between 4 and 6 kilograms, however those in South America may grow to be as heavy as 8 kilograms if they have the right nutrition. These enormous lizards may grow to be around 2 meters long from head to tail.

These reptiles, which are often referred to as green iguanas, really come in a variety of colors. The coloring of adults tends to grow more consistent with age, but the coloring of juveniles often seems more mottled or banded between green and brown. The color of a person's skin may change depending on a number of factors, including their mood, temperature, state of health, and social standing. These animals may be better able to regulate their body temperature thanks to the color change. Because the lizard's body temperature is lower in the morning, its skin color will become darker. This allows it to more effectively absorb heat from the sun. These animals, on the other hand, grow lighter or whiter when the hot midday sun shines onto them, which helps to reflect the sun's rays and minimizes the amount of heat that is absorbed. Iguanas who are more dominant in their habitat tend to have a darker coloration than iguanas that are lower on the dominance hierarchy. The vast majority of the color variety found in this species is shown by males, and some researchers believe that it is caused by sex hormones. It is possible for males to develop a brilliant orange or golden hue six to eight weeks before to courtship and while they are actively courting. Despite this, coloring is still associated to dominance position. The majority of mature females have their green coloration all throughout their lives.

Other characteristics that are unique to this species include a hanging dewlap below the throat, a dorsal crest composed of dermal spines that extend from the middle of the neck to the base of the tail, and a long tail that tapers toward the tip. Adult men tend to have a more pronounced dewlap than their female counterparts do. The leading edge of this structure, which is employed in territorial defense or when the animal is scared, is supported and stiffened by extensions of the hyoid bones. This structure is used when the animal is scared. When it is expanded, this fleshy structure also performs the function of absorbing heat and releasing it into the surrounding air.

The eyes that are laterally located are mostly covered by

an eyelid that is fixed in place, whereas the lower eyelid may move freely.

A parietal eye is located on the dorsal midline of the skull, behind the eyes, in between the parietal bones. Although it is not a genuine "eye," this sense organ acts as a meter for solar radiation and contributes to the development of sex organs, the thyroid gland, and endocrine glands. The visual impact of this so-called "eye" is mostly restricted to the detection of shadows cast by predators coming from above.

Habitat and diet

These iguanas used to occupy a much greater range on the southern coastlines of Jamaica back in the day, but currently the only place on the island where you can see them is in an area known as the Hellshire Hills. Iguanas are truly only able to be discovered in the most inaccessible parts of this dry forest that is full of rocky, limestone outcrops since it is regarded to be one of the most endangered ecosystems in the world.

Iguanas native to Jamaica have very long toes and keen claws, which allow them to climb up trees and feed on the leaves, fruit, and flowers there. Although plants make up the majority of the reptiles' meals, they will also consume snails, insects, and other small animals if they are accessible.

CHAPTER THREE

Reproduction

Following copulation, the female Jamaican iguana will begin excavating tunnels in order to investigate the chemical make-up of the surrounding soil. As each female hunts for the ideal location to deposit her eggs, excavations may begin a significant amount of time before the actual laying of the eggs. When she is ready, the female lays anything from six to twenty eggs in a clutch, which is then covered with sand and soil.

In contrast to sea turtles, who go back to the water once they have laid their eggs, the female iguana's job is not yet over. The female iguana will stay at the nesting place for up to two weeks to protect the eggs from being stolen by other female iguanas. Iguanas have a method of warding off potential threats that consists of extending a flap of skin known as a dewlap from behind their necks when they are approached. In the event that the other females do not get the message, however, the pregnant female will resort to biting and chasing other females in an attempt to protect her eggs from being disturbed.

Iguana hatchlings emerge from their eggs after an incubation period of 85 to 87 days and work their way to the surface using their sharp claws. Then, they have to do their best to make it on their own, which is a challenge that is made more manageable by the fact that the younger ones have a propensity to hide in the trees.

Information Regarding the Animal Shelter at Cub Creek

Housing - The Reptile Room is where all of our reptiles, including Chaos, are kept, including the rest of our lizards and snakes. He lives in a spacious cage that is managed for heat and UV light and is stuffed with fake plants to make it seem like their natural habitat in the tropics. He has access to clean water as well as a large number of hiding spots and areas to investigate and sun himself.

Diet: Because Chaos is still in the juvenile period of his development, he is provided with new food on a daily basis. In order to provide him with all of the essential nutrients he need in order to maintain his health, we offer him apple, shredded sweet potato, and chopped greens that have been fortified with calcium powder. In order to provide him with extra vitamins and minerals, we feed him a wide variety of fruits and vegetables.

Enrichment - The majority of the enrichment that we provide for our lizards comes from the fact that we handle them, socialize them, and house them in an enclosure with other species. They are handled on a daily basis throughout the summer months, and on occasion, when it is sufficiently warm, they are even taken outdoors. During the offseason, you may see Animal Interns working while carrying them about on their shoulders.

Practices and Methods of Living

Green iguanas are diurnal, arboreal reptiles. They are exceptionally nimble climbers, and lizards may survive falls of up to 15 meters (50 feet) in height without suffering any injuries (iguanas use their hind leg claws to clasp leaves and branches to break a fall). Iguanas del rio preferrán permanecer sobre la tierra in condiciones fras y lluvias para se mantener más cali These solitary lizards often make their homes close to bodies of water and are exceptional swimmers. Iguanas spend their whole time in the water underwater, with all four of their legs hanging loosely against their sides. They move through the water quickly and efficiently because to their strong tail strokes.

Iguanas will often freeze or hide when they perceive that they are under danger.

CHAPTER FOUR

Development

A female is ready to deposit her eggs around 65 days after she has been fertilized by a man. The size of the hen's eggs and the quantity of eggs she lays are both different from one another and rely on her nutritional state as well as her level of maturity. Eggs have a diameter of around 15.4 mm and range in length from 35 to 40 mm (Frye, 1995). An average of ten to thirty eggs with a leathery white or light cream hue are laid in a nest over the course of three days. The eggs have a leathery texture. Nests may be found anywhere from 45 centimeters to more than a meter deep, and in locations with a shortage of nesting grounds, they may be shared with other females. Females may return to the nest many times after depositing their eggs, but they do not remain to defend the nest after they leave.

The duration of the incubation period ranges from 90 to 120 days. The temperature need to be somewhere in the range of 85 and 91 degrees Fahrenheit. The newly hatched chicks crack open the egg using a specialized egg tooth known as the caruncle, which they lose soon after they emerge from the shell. The majority of an iguana's nutrition for the first week or two of its life comes from the yolk that it has digested.

The process of mating seems to include many females. The act of courting takes place inside a territorial boundary when there may be more than one female present. It's fairly unusual for men to fight with one another. Males engage in courtship behaviors such as head bobbing, extending and retracting the dewlap, nuzzling or biting a female's neck, and extending and retracting the dewlap. In addition to marking females, dominant males may use a waxy, pheromone-containing substance that is secreted from the pores in their femoral glands to mark rocks, branches, and other objects.

Dangers to one's ability to live

Within the small pockets of forest where they still exist, Jamaican iguanas must contend with a variety of dangers. Chief among these are invasive species like the mongoose, which preys on iguana eggs and young, as well as cats, which have been observed hunting and killing juvenile iguanas. Feral hogs may also be a problem, as they have been documented tearing up iguana nests on other islands. What's more, the dogs locals use to hunt hogs are dangerous, too, as one of the few animals on Jamaica that can take down a full grown iguana.

With just about 200 of the reptiles left in the wild, and all of those restricted to under four square miles of remote dry forests, the iguanas may be particularly susceptible to habitat loss, as well. Cutting down trees for use in the charcoal industry is an important source of income for the people who live near Jamaican iguanas, and this practice has already degraded as much as a third of the species' habitat, according to the International Union for Conservation of Nature (IUCN).

Some have also proposed opening the Hellshire Hills to other kinds of development, such as limestone mining, housing settlements, and tourism operations, all of which would further imperil these rare lizards. Diet and Nutrition

Iguanas verdes are herbivorous by nature and are a kind of reptile. They consume the leaves, flowers, fruit, and developing shoots of up to one hundred different plant species, including mustard greens, dandelion greens, and growing shoots. Adult Green iguanas living in the wild may consume grasshoppers, tree snails, and the eggs of birds.

The mating system of green iguanas is polygynandrous, which means they are promiscuous. This indicates that both men and females mate with more than one partner over their lifetime. The dry season is the time when the breeding season takes place. During this period, males have a propensity to show more dominant behaviors, such as bobbing their heads and lashing their tails. They also have a tendency to produce a dorsal crest that is higher than females do, as well as dorsal spines that are taller (or spikes). During a single, annual synchronized nesting session, females will lay a single clutch of anything from 20 to 71 eggs. After the eggs have been laid, they do not provide any more defense beyond protecting the nesting burrow while it is being excavated. After an incubation period of between 10 and 15 weeks, the young birds finally erupt from their eggs. Once they have hatched, baby iguanas have a coloration and form that are comparable to that of their parents. They resemble adult females more than adult males and do not have any dorsal spines. For the first year of their existence, juveniles are required to reside with their families. Green iguanas are the only species of reptile that do this, since the males of these groups often utilize their own bodies to shelter and defend the females from potential threats. In general, female Green Iguanas reach reproductive maturity between the ages of two and four years old.

CHAPTER FIVE

Population The dangers posed by population

The flesh and eggs of green iguanas have been used as a source of protein across their natural area for a significant amount of time. Additionally, green iguanas are highly coveted for the purported medicinal and aphrodisiacal capabilities that they possess. In addition, the hides of these lizards are employed in the production of leather. The worldwide commerce in pets has a significant negative impact on green iguana populations, as does the destruction of their natural habitat caused by human development and the use of land for grazing.

The number of the population

The Green Iguana is said to be locally abundant and widespread over its range, but there is no overall population estimate available, according to the International Union for Conservation of Nature

(IUCN). The current status of this species on the IUCN Red List is that it is considered to be of Least Concern (LC).

Ecological niche

These stunning lizards perform a very significant part in maintaining the health of the habitat in which they are found. Due to their nutrition, Green iguanas are particularly useful as seed dispersers. In addition, they are a species of prey for the local predators, including humans. Because reptiles are more sensitive to changes in their environments than people are, green iguanas may also serve as an indicator of these shifts in the natural world. People may thus be forewarned about potential issues before they grow to unacceptable proportions if their answers are monitored.

Domestication

Because of their placid temperament and vivid coloring, green iguanas are often kept as pets in homes that do not allow them to go free. The pet industry in the United States has created a significant demand for these lizards. Only in 1995, the United States took in 800,000 iguanas, the most majority of which came from zoos and other types of captive breeding facilities located in their respective home nations (Honduras, El Salvador, Colombia, and Panama). On the other hand, it may be difficult to properly care for these creatures throughout the course of their lives, and many of them pass away within a few years of being purchased.

Conservation

The fact that Jamaican iguanas may still be seen living in their natural habitat is celebrated as a victory for environmental protection in the modern day. This is due to the fact that the vast majority of specialists thought that the species had become extinct in the 1940s.

However, a lone sighting in 1970 by a hunter provided some evidence that the species hadn't completely vanished quite yet. Then, in 1990, there was still another sighting, which provided confirmation that Jamaican iguanas were still skulking about in the Hellshire Hills and prompted conservation efforts.

The first thing that needed to be done to save the iguanas was to shield them from the invading animals that may eat them. The mongoose population in the habitat of the reptile was assisted to decrease by extensive trapping operations, and the number of iguanas was further reinforced by the release of captive-bred iguanas, which allowed the population to increase to where it is now.

The Jamaican iguana is still regarded by the IUCN as belonging to the severely endangered species. The number of nesting females and yearly hatchlings grew more than six-fold between 1991 and 2013, according to surveys, which provides fresh hope for the species.

Some Endangered Iguana • CLASS: Reptilla (Reptiles) • ORDER: Squamata • FAMILY: Iguanidae • SUBFAMILY: Iguaninae • GENERA: 8 • SPECIES: 35 accepted as at this moment

Iguanas are among the biggest lizards that can be found in the Americas, and the whiplike tail that they have accounts for almost half of their total length. Iguanas, like other reptiles, are creatures that have a cold-blooded metabolism, produce eggs, and have a strong capacity to adapt to the environment in which they live.

There is a huge amount of variety among the species of iguana when it comes to size, color, behavior, and the degree to which they are threatened in the wild. Some, such as the green iguana, are extremely numerous, whilst others, such as the banded iguanas of Fiji, are on the verge of extinction. The desert iguana and the chuckwalla are the two species of iguanas that are indigenous to San Diego County.

CHAPTER SIX

HABITAT AND DIET

Because of the wide variety in appearance and behavior among the several species of iguana, it may be difficult to tell which ones belong to the same family. Although some iguanas have colors that are vibrant and dazzling, others have colors that are more muted and subdued. Iguanas live in such a diverse range of environments that each species has developed its own set of specialized adaptations.

The marine iguana that lives on the Galapagos Islands is an excellent swimmer, and its dark coloring allows it to quickly warm its body after venturing out into the chilly water.

On the other hand, the green iguana finds its natural habitat high in the treetops of a tropical rainforest. Other iguana species, on the other hand, have adapted in such a way that they are able to survive in the dry, scorching desert as well as rocky locations.

Iguanas in Fiji live in a variety of environments, from coastal marshes and lowland forests to rainforests on the slopes of Fiji's volcanoes. Their bodies are emerald green, and they have bands of white or blue across their backs, which are more pronounced on the males. They are very arboreal and have long tails and strong toes with sharp claws to help them maintain their balance when living in the trees.

Iguanas with bands are almost never observed on the ground because they migrate from tree to tree by exploiting the overlapping branches of the trees. They consume a wide variety of foods, including fruits, flowers, leaves, and even insects in their diet.

Adult banded iguanas may grow to be up to 21 inches (53 centimeters) long, with the tail accounting for more than half of that length. They reach complete maturity weighing anywhere from 99 to 199 grams, with males often being bigger and heavier than females. Their weight ranges from 3.5 to 7 ounces.

The Caribbean islands are home to more than 500 different species of reptiles, of which 94% are endemic to the region and cannot be found anywhere else on the planet. Rock iguanas are the aggregate name given to many different kinds of iguanas found in the Caribbean; some of these iguanas are only found on one or two islands. Each year, the female rock iguana lays a clutch of five to twenty eggs that are quite big. The larger eggs result in huge hatchlings, which developed as a consequence of their being a dearth of local predators. Iguanas that live on islands, as opposed to their mainland counterparts such as green iguanas, do not have the same pressure to have a large number of offspring in order to protect themselves from potential threats.

The Turks and Caicos iguanas are the smallest members of the species known as rock iguanas. They all consume a broad range of fruits and play a key role in the spread of seeds for many native plant species.

The vast majority of iguanas are herbivores, and their diets consist mostly of fruits, flower buds, and young leaves. Some even like the taste of a juicy mealworm or wax worm once in a while! In order to remove algae off rocks, marine iguanas must dive deep into the water.

Iguanas at the San Diego Zoo and San Diego Zoo Safari Park are given a fruit salad that consists of a range of fruits as well as dark leafy greens, and some of them are also given crickets, mealworms, and wax worms. However, since wax worms contain a significant amount of fat, they are placed in the "dessert" section of the menu.

Iguanas, themselves, are consumed by a wide range of natural predators, such as hawks, owls, and snakes, in addition to being consumed by humans. On farms in Central and South America, green iguanas are grown specifically for the purpose of being consumed by humans. Iguana hatchlings and juveniles are especially susceptible to being eaten by stray cats, and no iguana is secure from being attacked by a pack of dogs. The whiplike tail of the iguana may be used

for defense, and many species
have tails that are covered
with sharp "spines" that carry
an additional "punch."

CHAPTER SEVEN

FAMILY LIFE

There are three baby blue iguanas from the endangered Grand Cayman species.

The baby iguana does not have a mother: The females of most species of iguana excavate a burrow in a sunny spot, place their eggs within the hole, cover them, and then abandon the eggs to develop on their own. Even species of iguana that live in trees must go to the ground to reproduce. The temperature within the burrow is between 77 and 89 degrees Fahrenheit, and it seldom varies from that range (25 to 32 degrees Celsius). The eggs are allowed to hatch due to the warm temperature. There is a high probability that all of the eggs in a nest will hatch at the same time, and the young will emerge from their burrow without any assistance from their parents. Iguana hatchlings are exposed to a wide variety of threats while they are on their own.

AT THE ANIMAL HUT

Iguanas of several species may be seen residing at both the San Diego Zoo and the San Diego Zoo Safari Park. As we provide care for them, we get valuable knowledge about them, such as the perfect environmental circumstances for reproduction or their specific food requirements. We hope that the knowledge we get will allow us to improve the odds of iguanas surviving in their natural habitat. Over the years, we've had a lot of success when it comes to breeding animals. For example, the San Diego Zoo was the first zoo in the United States to successfully hatch an Anegada Island iguana egg.

The Zoo has a long history of working with Fiji Island banded iguanas, beginning with a gift of six of these lizards from the prince of Tonga in 1965, and we received our first hatchling in 1981. The Fiji Island banded iguana is found only in Fiji and the surrounding islands in the South Pacific. Today, the endangered species has the biggest and most successful colony of any location outside of Fiji other than the San Diego Zoo.

THE END